WHERE GOD IS AT HOME

OTHER COLLECTIONS OF POETRY
BY IRENE ZIMMERMAN

Convergence

For-Giving Ground

Woman Un-Bent

Incarnation

WHERE GOD IS AT HOME

Poems of God's Word and World
Illuminated by The Message®

IRENE ZIMMERMAN, OSF
Photographs by James Stephen Behrens, OCSO

WHERE GOD IS AT HOME
Poems of God's Word and World, Illuminated by The Message®
by Irene Zimmerman, OSF

Copyright © 2019 by Irene Zimmerman, School Sisters of St. Francis, Milwaukee, WI

Photographs © 2019 by James Stephen Behrens, OCSO

Scripture taken from *The Message: Catholic/Ecumenical Edition* Copyright © 2013 by Eugene H. Peterson. All rights reserved. Licensed with permission of NavPress. Represented by Tyndale House Publishers Inc. Carol Stream, Illinois 60188.

The Message and *The Message* logo are registered trademarks of NavPress. Used by permission. All rights reserved.

Published by ACTA Publications, 4848 N. Clark Street, Chicago, IL 60640, (800) 397-2282, www.actapublications.com

Library of Congress Number: 2019906520
ISBN: 978-0-87946-676-3
Printed in the United States of America by Total Printing Systems
Year 30 29 28 27 26 25 24 23 22 21 20 19
Printing 20 19 18 17 16 15 14 13 12 11 10 9 8 7 6 5 4 3 2

TABLE OF CONTENTS

DEDICATION

To the School Sisters of St. Francis
who taught and mentored me from first grade through college,
with special thanks to the sister musicians, artists, and poets
whose lives and works continue to inspire me

INTRODUCTION

More than a dozen years ago I had the strong desire and determination to write and present, in one volume, poems that celebrate Scripture and Creation—what medieval theologians referred to as God's two "books" of self-revelation. *Where God Is at Home: Poems of God's Word and World* is born of that desire.

The poems are greatly enhanced by relevant scriptural texts, making it truly a book for spiritual reading, as well as for enjoyment. The texts are taken from *The Message*, a popular translation of the Bible in lively, contemporary language done by Eugene H. Peterson, now available in a Catholic/Ecumenical Edition.

The book begins with poems inspired by scriptural stories, characters, and events. As did two of my earlier collections, *Woman Un-Bent* (Saint Mary's Press, 1999) and *Incarnation* (Cowley Publications, 2004, now an imprint of Rowman & Littlefield), these new poems are intended to help you imagine the scene and perhaps gain new insights into the biblical text. In addition, I hope that those of you who are prayer leaders and liturgical ministers will find them to be a helpful resource in your ministry.

The second part of *Where God Is at Home* stars God's creatures, including human ones. For many of us, creation is where we first encounter God. I began to experience something of the God-Mystery on the Iowa farm where I grew up. Breezes rustled the drying corn or moved across fragrant hay fields. Plants rooted, sprouted, bloomed, gave fragrance in spring and food in autumn in the form of apples, cherries, peaches, potatoes. The animals sharing the turf with me offered eggs, milk, butter, meat. They used their unique voices—they peeped, clucked, crowed, squawked, chirped, mewed, barked, mooed, whinnied, snorted—to tell me of God's creativity, generosity, humor, beauty.

"Nature cannot be regarded as something separate from ourselves or as a mere setting in which we live," writes Pope Francis in his immensely important *Laudato Si'.* "We are part of nature, included in it and thus in constant interaction with it" (139). As we grow in our awareness of God's creation, of our place in it, and of urgent responsibilities to care for it, we human beings are filled with wonder, joy, and gratitude.

Through these poems and texts celebrating God's Word and World, I invite you to join me in our unique human vocation—to use Rabbi Abraham Heschel's felicitous phrase—to be "cantors of the universe."

Irene Zimmerman, OSF
June 2019

MORE ABOUT THE MESSAGE®

The Message: Catholic/Ecumenical Edition by Eugene Peterson includes William Griffin's translation of deutero-canonical texts (the books of Judith, Tobit, Sirach, Wisdom, Baruch, 1 and 2 Maccabees, and additions to Esther and Daniel). One example of Griffin's deutero-canonical translation is the Book of Judith, the story of how the beautiful, holy, heroic widow Judith saved the Jewish people of Bethulia from being massacred by the Assyrians, referenced in the poem and passage on pages 24-26. For more on *The Message: Catholic/Ecumenical Edition* visit themessagecatholic.com.

GOD'S WORD

That day we learned
his most elementary lesson:
to fish for people
you have to put yourself
on the hook.
—from "Fi(ni)shing School"

GOD SPEAKS

and the Word
explodes into galaxies
streams into stars

plays on planets
swims in seas
dives with dolphins

bursts onto beaches
hikes up hills
wanders in woods

soughs with cedars
sings with sparrows
shouts with children

carves out a cave
enters a woman
becomes Flesh

lives among us
now
and forever

First this: God created the Heavens and Earth—all you see, all you don't see. Earth was a soup of nothingness, a bottomless emptiness, an inky blackness. God's Spirit brooded like a bird above the watery abyss.

> *God spoke: "Light!"*
> 　　*And light appeared.*
> *God saw that light was good*
> 　　*and separated light from dark.*
> *God named the light Day,*
> 　　*he named the dark Night.*
> *It was evening, it was morning—*
> *Day One.*

Genesis 1:1-5

ABRAHAM AND SARAH

Lying together
under the tent
of God's promise,
the laughing stars
playing hide-and-seek
just beyond reach—
how could they bear
to close their eyes?

*After all these things, this word of G*OD *came to Abram in a vision: "Don't be afraid, Abram. I'm your shield. Your reward will be grand!"*

*Abram said, "G*OD*, Master, what use are your gifts as long as I'm childless and Eliezer of Damascus is going to inherit everything?" Abram continued, "See, you've given me no children, and now a mere house servant is going to get it all."*

*Then G*OD*'s Message came: "Don't worry, he won't be your heir; a son from your body will be your heir."*

Then he took him outside and said, "Look at the sky. Count the stars. Can you do it? Count your descendants! You're going to have a big family, Abram!"

Genesis 15:1-5

The men said to him, "Where is Sarah your wife?"

He said, "In the tent."

One of them said, "I'm coming back about this time next year. When I arrive, your wife Sarah will have a son." Sarah was listening at the tent opening, just behind the man.

Abraham and Sarah were old by this time, very old. Sarah was far past the age for having babies. Sarah laughed within herself, "An old woman like me? Get pregnant? With this old man of a husband?"

*G*OD *said to Abraham, "Why did Sarah laugh saying, 'Me? Have a baby? An old woman like me?' Is anything too hard for G*OD*? I'll be back about this time next year and Sarah will have a baby."*

Genesis 18:9-14

SELLING JOSEPH

Elder brother Judah grabs
a rope of compromise
and dangles it before his brothers'
Joseph-jealous eyes:
Why not make a profit from
this murderous enterprise
and sell our bragging brother
into slavery?
They agree.

A caravan stands ready—
the camels on the road.
Young Joseph is delivered
from a twisted brotherhood
and his many-colored coat returned
to Jacob, soaked in blood.

When Joseph reached his brothers, they ripped off the fancy coat he was wearing, grabbed him, and threw him into a cistern. The cistern was dry; there wasn't any water in it.

Then they sat down to eat their supper. Looking up, they saw a caravan of Ishmaelites on their way from Gilead, their camels loaded with spices, ointments, and perfumes to sell in Egypt. Judah said, "Brothers, what are we going to get out of killing our brother and concealing the evidence? Let's sell him to the Ishmaelites, but let's not kill him—he is, after all, our brother, our own flesh and blood." His brothers agreed.

By that time the Midianite traders were passing by. His brothers pulled Joseph out of the cistern and sold him for twenty pieces of silver to the Ishmaelites who took Joseph with them down to Egypt....

They took Joseph's coat, butchered a goat, and dipped the coat in the blood. They took the fancy coat back to their father and said, "We found this. Look it over—do you think this is your son's coat?"

Genesis 37:23-28, 31-32

DAVID MEETS GOLIATH

When the roaring boast burst forth
from the giant Philistine's mouth,
all Israel knew their final hour had come—

all but you, ruddy young David, savior
of your father's sheep from lion and bear,

struck now by the sudden, brash belief
slung straight at you by God—

belief in the saving power
of five smooth stones
lying in the wadi at your feet.

"Master," said David, "don't give up hope. I'm ready to go and fight this Philistine."

Saul answered David, "You can't go and fight this Philistine. You're too young and inexperienced—and he's been at this fighting business since before you were born."

David said, "I've been a shepherd, tending sheep for my father. Whenever a lion or bear came and took a lamb from the flock, I'd go after it, knock it down, and rescue the lamb. If it turned on me, I'd grab it by the throat, wring its neck, and kill it. Lion or bear, it made no difference—I killed it. And I'll do the same to this Philistine pig who is taunting the troops of God-Alive. God, who delivered me from the teeth of the lion and the claws of the bear, will deliver me from this Philistine."

Saul said, "Go. And God help you!"...

Then David took his shepherd's staff, selected five smooth stones from the brook, and put them in the pocket of his shepherd's pack, and with his sling in his hand approached Goliath.

1 Samuel 17:32-37, 40

HOW JUDITH SAVED HER PEOPLE

When the Elders of Bethulia met on the assembly floor
and decided to surrender in five days more
unless the Lord God saved them, the widow Judith prayed
in her rooftop hermitage where she had mostly stayed
for three mournful years, since her husband had died.
Resolutely now, she laid her widow's weeds aside.
O Holy One, she pleaded, grant me courage and power
to save your people Israel from this dreadful hour.

That night she donned her jewels, called her maid, and went
to the camp of the Assyrians where soldiers led them to the tent
of Holofernes. Her beauty smote the General right between the eyes.
There's no woman in the world, he thought, more beautiful and wise.
God sent me, said Judith, to achieve great things with you.
Little did he comprehend just how her words were true.

For three days and nights the women freely wandered in and out.
By day four, Holofernes seethed in a mighty pout.
He exclaimed to his eunuch, *This is a disgrace.*
If I don't seduce her soon, she will scorn me to my face!

At that evening's banquet, Judith wound alluring wiles
around her salivating host as he feasted on her smiles
and called loudly for wine, and more of it, and more.
He drank more wine that night than he had ever drunk before.
At last, besotted, befuddled, he led her to his tent.
His tired servants took one look and discreetly went.

Daintily, she dawdled with ties and countless bows
while he waited lustfully for her to shed her clothes.
But sleep at last conquered him and he commenced to snore.
This was, of course, exactly what she had been praying for.
At once she grabbed the General's sword which hung above the bed
and cut off, with two mighty strokes, Holofernes' head.

The sleepy, unsuspecting guards didn't think to sound alarm
when Judith and her handmaid walked with beauty and charm
out the gates of the Assyrian camp, their gory treasure rolled
in Holofernes' canopy of purple fringed with gold.

In Bethulia at that time there lived a widow named Judith.... Her husband was Mannasseh, from the same tribe and lineage; he died during a barley harvest....

That was three years, four months earlier.

Judith remained in her home, mostly in the living area on the roof, where she erected an airy, breezy prayer tent for herself.... She kept the widow's fast.

As for Judith's reputation, no one could lay a finger on her because she was a God-fearing person. She'd heard about the rough words spoken to Uzziah and the other elders of the city. And she'd heard his response—that he swore he'd hand the town over to the Assyrians in five days....

Judith 8:1-10

JONAH THINKS THINGS OVER

If I had a choice I would wish
for a ride more commodious
and much less odious
than the belly of a fish!

However, I have to admit
when this "ship" showed up from the pit
just as the waters closed in
to drown me and my sin,

I didn't stop for a minute
to check how much room was in it.

Then Jonah prayed to his God from the belly of the fish. He prayed:
"In trouble, deep trouble, I prayed to God.
  He answered me.
From the belly of the grave I cried, 'Help!'
  You heard my cry....
Ocean gripped me by the throat.
  The ancient Abyss grabbed me and held tight.
My head was all tangled in seaweed
  at the bottom of the sea where the mountains take root.
I was as far down as a body can go,
  and the gates were slamming shut behind me forever—
Yet you pulled me up from that grave alive,
  O God, *my God!*
When my life was slipping away,
  I remembered God,
And my prayer got through to you,
  made it all the way to your Holy Temple.
Those who worship hollow gods, god-frauds,
  walk away from their only true love.
But I'm worshiping you, God,
  calling out in thanksgiving!
And I'll do what I promised I'd do!
  Salvation belongs to God!"

Jonah 2:1-2, 5-9

CONSIDERING THE BABEL FABLE

The people of Babel
built a fabulous tower.
Why?
Because they were able
and wanted the power
to lord over the sky.

Their lilliputian intrusion
into limitless blue overhead
brought about a profusion
of lingual confusion instead.

Two ways to read this: Ridicule
and label as *fool*
the people of Babel.
Or go to the table
and work toward consensus
to avoid like consequences.

Then they said, "Come, let's build ourselves a city and a tower that reaches Heaven. Let's make ourselves famous so we won't be scattered here and there across the Earth."

GOD came down to look over the city and the tower those people had built.

GOD took one look and said, "One people, one language; why, this is only a first step. No telling what they'll come up with next—they'll stop at nothing! Come, we'll go down and garble their speech so they won't understand each other." Then GOD scattered them from there all over the world. And they had to quit building the city. That's how it came to be called Babel, because there GOD turned their language into "babble." From there GOD scattered them all over the world.

Genesis 11:4-9

THE MESSENGER

God had made it clear to Gabriel
that the whole plan hinged upon
the maiden's uncoerced consent,
and so, intent that there should be
no witness in the dreadful event
that her answer would be *No*,
the angel hid behind the garden wall,
practicing the message he'd been sent
to give and waiting till she was alone
before he made his awesome presence known.

Even when her mother came outside
and sat and napped in morning's cooling shade,
the angel hesitated, not wishing to intrude
and frighten Mary in her solitude
(so he told himself). But when at last he stood
before God's chosen one, face to face,
he knew that he need not have been afraid
and greeted her with every blessed accolade,
dazzled by her plenitude of grace.

In the sixth month of Elizabeth's pregnancy, God sent the angel Gabriel to the Galilean village of Nazareth to a virgin engaged to be married to a man descended from David. His name was Joseph, and the virgin's name, Mary.

Luke 1:26-27

ANNUNCIATION

God sent Gabriel down
to Mary, a little nobody
in the little nothing-town
of Nazareth in Galilee

to obtain her consent
to be the mother of God's Son—
a mission without precedent
in the annals of angeldom.

Gabriel filled the tiny space
as he grandly greeted her:
Hail Mary, full of grace.
You are to be God's mother!

Though startled and afraid
at the strange apparition,
the young, courageous maid
dared to ask her question:

I haven't been with any man,
she said, *How can this be?*
The angel answered, *The Holy One*
knows no impossibility,

and continued in the same breath
to give Mary the good news
that her elder cousin Elizabeth
was already six months in recluse.

Hearing this, the young mother-to-be
gracefully bowed and said:
Amen. So let it be done to me.
Back to heaven Gabriel sped.

In less than the space of a breath,
down to earth the Holy One came.
Since that day in Nazareth,
nothing has been the same.

Upon entering, Gabriel greeted her:

> Good morning!
> You're beautiful with God's beauty,
> Beautiful inside and out!
> God be with you.

She was thoroughly shaken, wondering what was behind a greeting like that. But the angel assured her, "Mary, you have nothing to fear. God has a surprise for you: You will become pregnant and give birth to a son and call his name Jesus.

> He will be great,
>   be called 'Son of the Highest.'
> The Lord God will give him
>   the throne of his father David;
> He will rule Jacob's house forever—
>   no end, ever, to his kingdom."

Mary said to the angel, "But how? I've never slept with a man." The angel answered,

> The Holy Spirit will come upon you,
>   the power of the Highest hover over you;

> Therefore, the child you bring to birth
>> will be called Holy, Son of God.

"And did you know that your cousin Elizabeth conceived a son, old as she is? Everyone called her barren, and here she is six months' pregnant! Nothing, you see, is impossible with God."
And Mary said,

> Yes, I see it all now:
>> I'm the Lord's maid, ready to serve.
> Let it be with me
>> just as you say.

Then the angel left her.

Luke 1:28-38

ON THE WAY

(for the Feast of Visitation)

> She is carrying God's child
> (the weightiest mother-lode
> ever given a woman to bear)
> to Jerusalem,
> and her back is killing her
> as she rides the stony road
> on the donkey's bony back.
>
> Someday the son she carries
> will walk the stony way
> out of Jerusalem,
> carrying on his back
> a load that will kill him.

Mary didn't waste a minute. She got up and traveled to a town in Judah in the hill country, straight to Zechariah's house, and greeted Elizabeth.

Luke 1:39-40

MARY ARRIVES AT THE HOUSE OF ZECHARIAH

Now, Zechariah
of the tied tongue,
after six months
of apprenticeship
to stillness
while listening
to Elizabeth
happily humming
between bouts
of morning sickness,

now let the seed
of God's amazing grace
break open in you,
grow like wheat
from the sacred soil
of women sharing
the work and wonder
of child-bearing.

When Elizabeth heard Mary's greeting, the baby in her womb leaped. She was filled with the Holy Spirit, and sang out exuberantly,

> *You're so blessed among women,*
> *and the babe in your womb, also blessed!*

Mary stayed with Elizabeth for three months and then went back to her own home.

Luke 1:41-42, 56

OF ANGELS AND SHEEP

We shepherds woke to a sky
filled with shimmering light.
Singing sweet as milk and honey
poured down on us and our flock:

> *A Child is born*
> *to you this night,*
> *the promised One,*
> *your Savior.*
> *He's in a barn*
> *in Bethlehem,*
> *lying in a manger.*

We stood gaping, awestruck,
but the sheep trotted off
on a path of light, baaing to us
till we followed like lambs
to the stable.

There were sheepherders camping in the neighborhood. They had set night watches over their sheep. Suddenly, God's angel stood among them and God's glory blazed around them. They were terrified. The angel said, "Don't be afraid. I'm here to announce a great and joyful event that is meant for everybody, worldwide: A Savior has just been born in David's town, a Savior who is Messiah and Master. This is what you're to look for: a baby wrapped in a blanket and lying in a manger."

At once the angel was joined by a huge angelic choir singing God's praises:

> *Glory to God in the heavenly heights,*
> *Peace to all men and women on earth who please him.*

Luke 2:8-14

GIFT EXCHANGE

It was just as the angels had said:
in a lantern's dim light
the shepherds saw
a man and a woman gazing
toward a manger where,
instead of oats and hay,
a newborn baby lay!

Barely had they realized
they'd come without a gift,
when the shepherds saw, surprised,
their newborn lamb wiggle-wobbling
between the thin bellies
of donkey and ox
straight to the animals' feedbox.

Steadying its legs, the lamb
pushed its woolly head inside
and warmly breathed
on the Lamb of God—
a perfect gift
for the newborn Lord
who'd come to save the world.

As the angel choir withdrew into heaven, the sheepherders talked it over. "Let's get over to Bethlehem as fast as we can and see for ourselves what God has revealed to us." They left, running, and found Mary and Joseph, and the baby lying in the manger.

Luke 2:15-16

BETHLEHEM MASSACRE

When Herod's spies returned
and told him that the travelers
had knelt to honor the child,
the wily ruler understood
that men monied enough
to come by camel
from a distant land
would not have gotten down
from their high seats
to kneel in the stink
of a sheep barn
for anyone less than a king.

By morning the streets of Bethlehem
ran with baby blood.

Herod, when he realized that the scholars had tricked him, flew into a rage. He commanded the murder of every little boy two years old and under who lived in Bethlehem and its surrounding hills. (He determined that age from information he'd gotten from the scholars.) That's when Jeremiah's sermon was fulfilled:

> *A sound was heard in Ramah,*
> *weeping and much lament.*
> *Rachel weeping for her children,*
> *Rachel refusing all solace,*
> *her children gone,*
> *dead and buried.*

Matthew 2:16-18

THE BOY JESUS ON HIS WAY TO BECOMING

They were out of the crowded city now.
The silence grew loud between them.
Jesus glanced at his mother, riding their donkey,
and saw hurt and weariness still on her face.

Sadness for the pain he had caused his parents
wrestled with his longing to share with them
his joy as he'd spoken with the teachers, asking
and answering questions with a wisdom
he had not known he possessed.

The road ahead seemed to stretch as endless
as the coming years of helping his father
carve wood into cupboards, tables, and chairs.
He fought the desire that rose in him—he wanted
to begin his future work now, not to have to wait!

He felt Joseph's quieting hand on his shoulder,
saw a reassuring look on his mother's face, and knew
they understood. He took deep breaths of the late
morning air as he shifted the burden of growing
squarely on obedient shoulders.

The next day they found Jesus in the Temple seated among the teachers, listening to them and asking questions. The teachers were all quite taken with him, impressed with the sharpness of his answers. But his parents were not impressed; they were upset and hurt.

His mother said, "Young man, why have you done this to us? Your father and I have been half out of our minds looking for you."

He said, "Why were you looking for me? Didn't you know that I had to be here, dealing with the things of my Father?" But they had no idea what he was talking about.

So he went back to Nazareth with them, and lived obediently with them. His mother held these things dearly, deep within herself. And Jesus matured, growing up in both body and spirit, blessed by both God and people.

Luke 2:46-52

SCAPEGOAT

After reading Isaiah,
Jesus rolled up the scroll,
gave it to the attendant,
and sat down.

The eyes of his hometown
watched, waited
for him to expound
on the prophet's promises.

The passage had often been read
to them; was there anything new
to be said, they wondered.
A child stirred, was stilled.

The strong voice of Jesus
broke open the egg of silence:
This day the prophecy is fulfilled.
I am the one of whom Isaiah spoke.

The people sat stunned.
Then whispers began:
Did you hear…? Did he say…?
Mary's son! Could he be…?

The town bully stood up and shouted:
Hey, who does he think he is?
He's nothing. Nobody.
He's just the carpenter's kid!

He raised a melee,
relentlessly goading the others until
they ran the kid out of town
and up to the crown of the Hill.

Jesus came to Nazareth where he had been reared. As he always did on the Sabbath, he went to the meeting place. When he stood up to read, he was handed the scroll of the prophet Isaiah. Unrolling the scroll, he found the place where it was written,

> *God's Spirit is on me;*
>> *he's chosen me to preach the Message of good news to the poor,*
> *Sent me to announce pardon to prisoners and*
>> *recovery of sight to the blind,*
> *To set the burdened and battered free,*
>> *to announce, "This is God's year to act!"*

He rolled up the scroll, handed it back to the assistant, and sat down. Every eye in the place was on him, intent. Then he started in, "You've just heard Scripture make history. It came true just now in this place."

All who were there, watching and listening, were surprised at how well he spoke. But they also said, "Isn't this Joseph's son, the one we've known since he was a youngster?"

He answered, "I suppose you're going to quote the proverb, 'Doctor, go heal yourself. Do here in your hometown what we heard you did in Capernaum.' Well, let me tell you something: No prophet is ever welcomed in his hometown…."

That set everyone in the meeting place seething with anger. They threw him out, banishing him from the village, then took him to a mountain cliff at the edge of the village to throw him to his doom.

Luke 4:16-24, 28-30

"DAUGHTER" HE CALLS ME

My daughter up with me all night.
A burden to her and Simon.
This old bag of bones.
No good for anyone anymore.
Time for me to die.

A strange man, this Jesus.
Simon so drawn to him.
What will we do
if he and Andrew
leave us to follow him?

They're coming!
My daughter asleep
and I with no strength
to get up to serve them.
It shames me.

Daughter, open your eyes.
Get up!
"Daughter" he calls me.
How strong his hands,
raising me up.

It is indeed as Simon said:
when this man speaks,
one wants to obey;
one wants to serve him,
even to rise from the dead.

Simon's mother-in-law was sick in bed, burning up with fever. They told Jesus. He
went to her, took her hand, and raised her up. No sooner had the fever left than she
was up fixing dinner for them.

Mark 1:30-31

MOVING ON

Jesus watched the glowing joy on her face
as Simon's mother-in-law served fresh-baked bread
and fruit in season, and filled cups again and again
with their finest wine till the house swam with laughter
and curious children from all over Capernaum
piled in through the open doorway.

News of her healing poured down dusty streets.
After sundown the whole city gathered at the door.
Cripples arrived, the tap of their crutches
guiding the blind. Soon the yard was flooded
with litters of the sick. As Jesus waded in,
touching each one, healing leaped from his hands.

Early next morning while it was still dark,
he arose from restless sleep, stole past the sprawling
disciples, and walked to a deserted place to pray.
Stars stood by as he wrestled with dark angels
who relentlessly showed him the pitiful procession
of human suffering that longed for his coming:

Widows stretched out bony arms and fingers,
the lame and blind begged with starving eyes,
lepers stumbled toward him on stumps of feet,
a Canaanite woman brought her dying daughter.
Meantime Pharisees plotted to catch him
and demons screamed, "We know who you are!"

His fisher followers found him at dawn
and announced with eager, naive pride: "Everyone
is looking for you!" (It could have been so easy.)
But he hauled in the net of the long night's
discernment: "We must tell the good news
to neighboring towns. Let us move on."

That evening, after the sun was down, they brought sick and evil-afflicted people to him, the whole city lined up at his door! He cured their sick bodies and tormented spirits. Because the demons knew his true identity, he didn't let them say a word.

While it was still night, way before dawn, he got up and went out to a secluded spot and prayed. Simon and those with him went looking for him. They found him and said, "Everybody's looking for you."

Jesus said, "Let's go to the rest of the villages so I can preach there also. This is why I've come."

Mark 1:32-38

MARY'S SECOND RITE OF PASSAGE I

The awkward silence spoke loudly
as Mary approached the village well.
What news of her son had they heard now,
she wondered. She soon learned,
as they resumed their quiet talking.

Anna confided: *My Jacob said*
he eats with sinners and tax collectors.
And yesterday he allowed his disciples
to pick grain on the Sabbath....
Our Elders are watching him.

Esther spoke in his defense: *People come*
day and night, expecting miracles.
He's getting no rest. Some men even tore
a hole in his roof and let down a paralytic.
He healed the man, but the hole is still there.

Mary of Cleophas took Mary aside.
My Joses said Jesus is out of his mind.
You must talk to him. He's your firstborn son.
The Torah tells us to honor our parents.
He ought to be home to take care of you.

Before Jesus had left, they'd talked about his mission.
She'd understood he'd heard the call and had to go.
But she knew, too, how the family hated gossip.
And now he had roused the elders' anger....
Yes, she must go to him, must warn him.

When they reached Capernaum, sweaty and tired,
they couldn't get through the crowd.
A man who knew them pushed his way to Jesus.
Your mother, brothers, and sisters are outside,
he said, waiting to see you.

Jesus came home and, as usual, a crowd gathered—so many making demands on him that there wasn't even time to eat. His friends heard what was going on and went to rescue him, by force if necessary. They suspected he was getting carried away with himself.

Mark 3:20-21

MARY'S SECOND RITE OF PASSAGE II

From where she stood, Mary heard
her son's loud cry: *My family
is waiting outside, you say?*

*But I say: You are my family now.
Whoever does the will of God
is my brother and sister and mother.*

Could she in all her pondering—
as she had carried her unborn son
from Nazareth to Bethlehem

and now as she'd carried her tired bones
from Nazareth to Capernaum
to bring him home from his madness—

could she have guessed
that she would be asked to let
the umbilical cord be cut a second time?

We hear her anguished cry:
Amen. So let it be done to me!
even at this distance.

Just then his mother and brothers showed up. Standing outside, they relayed a message that they wanted a word with him. He was surrounded by the crowd when he was given the message, "Your mother and brothers and sisters are outside looking for you."

Jesus responded, "Who do you think are my mother and brothers?" Looking around, taking in everyone seated around him, he said, "Right here, right in front of you—my mother and my brothers. Obedience is thicker than blood. The person who obeys God's will is my brother and sister and mother."

Mark 3:31-35

FI(NI)SHING SCHOOL

It made no sense.
Fish didn't bite at that time of day.
A carpenter's son from Nazareth—
what would he know about fishing?
Yet the command in his voice
sent us out to sea again.

After the catch we followed him.
I'll make you fishers of people, he said.
For three years we watched him
hauling in sinners, the blind and lame,
the deaf and dumb, those possessed
of evil spirits, those dispossessed.

One late afternoon when we were far
from any town, we asked Jesus
to dismiss the crowd—they numbered
in the thousands and all we had to offer
were a few loaves and fish.
Feed them yourselves, he said.

That day we learned
his most elementary lesson:
to fish for people
you have to put yourself
on the hook.

When Jesus finished teaching, he said to Simon, "Push out into deep water and let your nets out for a catch."

Simon said, "Master, we've been fishing hard all night and haven't caught even a minnow. But if you say so, I'll let out the nets." It was no sooner said than done—a huge haul of fish, straining the nets past capacity. They waved to their partners in the other boat to come help them. They filled both boats, nearly swamping them with the catch....

Jesus said to Simon, "There is nothing to fear. From now on you'll be fishing for men and women." They pulled their boats up on the beach, left them, nets and all, and followed him.

Luke 5:4-7, 10-11

At about this same time Jesus again found himself with a hungry crowd on his hands. He called his disciples together and said, "This crowd is breaking my heart. They have stuck with me for three days, and now they have nothing to eat. If I send them home hungry, they'll faint along the way—some of them have come a long distance."

His disciples responded, "What do you expect us to do about it? Buy food out here in the desert?"

He asked, "How much bread do you have?"

"Seven loaves," they said.

So Jesus told the crowd to sit down on the ground. After giving thanks, he took the seven bread loaves, broke them into pieces, and gave them to his disciples so they could hand them out to the crowd. They also had a few fish. He pronounced a blessing over the fish and told his disciples to hand them out as well.

Mark 8:1-7

A DISCIPLE REFLECTS ON THE TEMPEST

What I had failed to notice before,
as I remembered my fear of the demon's roar,
the impending crush of our boat in its paw,
and the imminent end of us all in its maw,

was how tired Jesus was—how he needed his rest
and had learned, in order to be at his best
when crowds besieged him, to sleep between shores,
lulled by the up-down-over of oars,

and was trying to teach us in turn to do this—
to rest in the trough between watery cliffs,
knowing tempests, however ferocious, cannot
escape the confines of God's teapot.

A huge storm came up. Waves poured into the boat, threatening to sink it. And Jesus was in the stern, head on a pillow, sleeping! They roused him, saying, "Teacher, is it nothing to you that we're going down?"

Awake now, he told the wind to pipe down and said to the sea, "Quiet! Settle down!" The wind ran out of breath; the sea became smooth as glass.

Mark 4:37-39

FRINGE BENEFIT

She wasn't supposed to be there.
She was unclean!
Nevertheless, she darted in, unseen,
to touch the fringe
of the seamless robe
his mother had made for him.

Who touched me? she heard
and fearfully confessed the deed,
for which she was blessed
by one soon to be, like her,
despised,
ostracized.

In the crowd that day there was a woman who for twelve years had been afflicted with hemorrhages. She had spent every penny she had on doctors but not one had been able to help her. She slipped in from behind and touched the edge of Jesus' robe. At that very moment her hemorrhaging stopped. Jesus said, "Who touched me?"

When no one stepped forward, Peter said, "But Master, we've got crowds of people on our hands. Dozens have touched you."

Jesus insisted, "Someone touched me. I felt power discharging from me."

When the woman realized that she couldn't remain hidden, she knelt trembling before him. In front of all the people, she blurted out her story—why she touched him and how at that same moment she was healed.

Jesus said, "Daughter, you took a risk trusting me, and now you're healed and whole. Live well, live blessed!"

Luke 8:43-48

TALITHA KOUM!

She was running
through tunneled darkness
toward dazzling light
when she felt warm breath on her face
and heard a voice filled with music
calling her back: *Talitha koum!*

When she opened her eyes
and saw astonished joy
lighting up her parents' tears,
she knew she still belonged
with them and obediently ate
the food they brought her.

In the days and years that followed,
they did not ask her
what she had seen and heard.
For this she was grateful.
She did not want to hurt them.
She loved them even more.

Yet all her life she remembered
and longed for the day
when she would hear the voice again
calling her, *Talitha koum!*
and she would be free
to run all the way to the light.

Everyone was crying and carrying on over her. Jesus said, "Don't cry. She didn't die; she's sleeping." They laughed at him. They knew she was dead.

Then Jesus, gripping her hand, called, "My dear child, get up." She was up in an instant, up and breathing again! He told them to give her something to eat. Her parents were ecstatic, but Jesus warned them to keep quiet. "Don't tell a soul what happened in this room."

Luke 8:52-56

LET THE CHILDREN COME TO ME

Little ones are like raw dough.
Knead love in their hearts
and watch them grow.

The people brought children to Jesus, hoping he might touch them. The disciples shooed them off. But Jesus was irate and let them know it: "Don't push these children away. Don't ever get between them and me. These children are at the very center of life in the kingdom. Mark this: Unless you accept God's kingdom in the simplicity of a child, you'll never get in." Then, gathering the children up in his arms, he laid his hands of blessing on them.

Mark 10:13-16

BREAD AT BETHANY

The scent of cinnamon and cloves spicing
the path led the disciples by the nose
to the home of Martha, Mary, and Lazarus.
It was nearing the sixth hour.
They hadn't eaten since sunrise.

Once inside, they hardly noticed when
Jesus called Mary, hovering at the door,
to *Come sit with us*. They'd been with him
long enough to know that women
were welcome in his circle of disciples.

But Martha noticed, and it wasn't long
before she burst into the room, her angry
Jesus, tell Mary to come and help me!
clashing incongruously with the homey
baking smells that rose from her clothing.

Jesus kneaded Martha's temper with a firm
but gentle *Martha, Martha*, assuring her
that her cinnamon loaves would satisfy their hunger.
Did she sit at his feet with her sister then
and learn to wait for the Bread to rise?

As they continued their travel, Jesus entered a village. A woman by the name of Martha welcomed him and made him feel quite at home. She had a sister, Mary, who sat before the Master, hanging on every word he said. But Martha was pulled away by all she had to do in the kitchen. Later, she stepped in, interrupting them. "Master, don't you care that my sister has abandoned the kitchen to me? Tell her to lend me a hand."

The Master said, "Martha, dear Martha, you're fussing far too much and getting yourself worked up over nothing. One thing only is essential, and Mary has chosen it—it's the main course, and won't be taken from her."

Luke 10:38-42

LOST SHEEP

Climbing too high,
trying to reach the sky
all by itself,
now caught on a shelf
of a sheer rock cliff,
it looks down, stiff
with sheepish alarm,
bleats for the arms
of the watchful Master
and safe green pasture.

The Pharisees and religion scholars were not pleased, not at all pleased. They growled, "He takes in sinners and eats meals with them, treating them like old friends." Their grumbling triggered this story.

"Suppose one of you had a hundred sheep and lost one. Wouldn't you leave the ninety-nine in the wilderness and go after the lost one until you found it? When found, you can be sure you would put it across your shoulders, rejoicing, and when you got home call in your friends and neighbors, saying, 'Celebrate with me! I've found my lost sheep!'"

Luke 15:2-6

INSIGHT

When Jesus gifted
Bartimaeus with sight,
the man saw and believed
in Unblinding Light.

Those who insisted
that they could see
walked away
blindly.

They called the man back a second time—the man who had been blind—and told him, "Give credit to God. We know this man is an impostor."

He replied, "I know nothing about that one way or the other. But I know one thing for sure: I was blind…I now see."

They said, "What did he do to you? How did he open your eyes?"

"I've told you over and over and you haven't listened. Why do you want to hear it again? Are you so eager to become his disciples?"

With that they jumped all over him. "You might be a disciple of that man, but we're disciples of Moses."

John 9:24-28

Like the blind, we inch along a wall,
groping eyeless in the dark.
We shuffle our way in broad daylight,
like the dead, but somehow walking.

Isaiah 59:10

ENTRANCE

On this first day of the week
everything is washed clean
in a rain of sunshine.

Hands reach out
to calm a skittish colt
bewildered by its burden.

The Son of David
rides a rainbowed road
that rocks with hosannas.

They brought the colt to Jesus. Then, throwing their coats on its back, they helped Jesus get on. As he rode, the people gave him a grand welcome, throwing their coats on the street.

Right at the crest, where Mount Olives begins its descent, the whole crowd of disciples burst into enthusiastic praise over all the mighty works they had witnessed:

> Blessed is he who comes,
>> the king in God's name!
> All's well in heaven!
>> Glory in the high places!

Luke 19:35-38

BETRAYAL

The maid calling you a liar,
and you, Peter, caught by the fire
with the lie showing
(after three years of knowing)
in the Galilean twist
of your tongue as you insist:
Don't know him!
Don't know him!

The fire climbing
the walls of the sky,
its fingers writing:
It's a lie! A lie!

Nowhere now, nowhere to go
to escape the rooster's crow
tattling up and down
every street in town:
Disaster! Disaster!
He betrayed the Master!

Arresting Jesus, they marched him off and took him into the house of the Chief Priest. Peter followed, but at a safe distance. In the middle of the courtyard some people had started a fire and were sitting around it, trying to keep warm. One of the serving maids sitting at the fire noticed him, then took a second look and said, "This man was with him!"

He denied it, "Woman, I don't even know him."

A short time later, someone else noticed him and said, "You're one of them."

But Peter denied it: "Man, I am not."

About an hour later, someone else spoke up, really adamant: "He's got to have been with him! He's got 'Galilean' written all over him."

Peter said, "Man, I don't know what you're talking about." At that very moment, the last word hardly off his lips, a rooster crowed. Just then, the Master turned and looked at Peter. Peter remembered what the Master had said to him: "Before the rooster crows, you will deny me three times." He went out and cried and cried and cried.

Luke 22:54-62

JESUS COMFORTS THE WOMEN (STATION 8)

Even as we cried for him,
he tried to console us.

Dear friends, I'll be all right,
he said, *I've come this far.*
I can see the end now,

and added, as blood spurted
from his thorn-crowned head,
blinding his eyes,

But you must be strong.
Your passion is yet to come.

When his voice choked
on the sweat and blood
rivering down his face,

we cried afresh
as we tried to assure him
that we'd be all right.

A huge crowd of people followed, along with women weeping and carrying on. At one point Jesus turned to the women and said, "Daughters of Jerusalem, don't cry for me. Cry for yourselves and for your children. The time is coming when they'll say, 'Lucky the women who never conceived! Lucky the wombs that never gave birth! Lucky the breasts that never gave milk!' Then they'll start calling to the mountains, 'Fall down on us!' calling to the hills, 'Cover us up!' If people do these things to a live, green tree, can you imagine what they'll do with deadwood?"

Luke 23:27-31

JESUS FALLS (STATION 9)

If I were in his place,
I'd call it quits this time.
I'd make the soldiers

beat me to death
where fewer could see
and ridicule.

But he's going to get up
and go on.
I can see it in his eyes.

Hold off your whips, men.
He doesn't need
our goading.

Now he's fitting his back
to the beam.
He's getting to his knees.

There's nothing ahead for him
except crucifixion.
What's that to live for?

What kind of man is this?
What gives him the will
to rise again?

When the captain there saw what happened, he honored God: "This man was
innocent! A good man, and innocent!"

Luke 23:47

THE PRIZE

Did
the
soldiers
gambling beneath the Cross
for the seamless robe
notice
the torn
body
hanging
from
nails
like a
garment?

And they nailed him to the cross. They divided up his clothes and threw dice to see who would get them.

They nailed him up at nine o'clock in the morning.

Mark 15:24-25

GOD'S GAMBLE

Hammer blows still echoing, soldiers
toss the dice, eager for the prize—
a seamless tunic made by Mary-love.

A loud cry rings out: *It is finished!*

Abruptly, daylight flips to night.
Earth itself upchucks the awful deed.
A soldier kneels on bloody stones, exclaims

Truly, this man was the Son of God!

Above them, the ripped, torn body
of the garment's wearer hangs unfurled—
God's winning gamble for the world.

But Jesus, again crying out loudly, breathed his last.

At that moment, the Temple curtain was ripped in two, top to bottom. There was an earthquake, and rocks were split in pieces. What's more, tombs were opened up, and many bodies of believers asleep in their graves were raised. (After Jesus' resurrection, they left the tombs, entered the holy city, and appeared to many.)

The captain of the guard and those with him, when they saw the earthquake and everything else that was happening, were scared to death. They said, "This has to be the Son of God!"

Matthew 27:50-54

JESUS DIES (STATION 12)

He hangs high
between earth and sky,
waiting to die.

Some play games.
Some call him names.
Some stand by.

Where am I?

People passing along the road jeered, shaking their heads in mock lament: "You bragged that you could tear down the Temple and then rebuild it in three days—so show us your stuff! Save yourself! If you're really God's Son, come down from that cross!"

The high priests, along with the religion scholars, were right there mixing it up with the rest of them, having a great time poking fun at him: "He saved others—but he can't save himself! Messiah, is he? King of Israel? Then let him climb down from that cross. We'll all become believers then!" Even the men crucified alongside him joined in the mockery.

Mark 15:29-32

While the soldiers were looking after themselves, Jesus' mother, his aunt Mary the wife of Clopas, and Mary Magdalene stood at the foot of the cross.

John 19:24

PIETÀ (STATION 13)

My Son, my Son,
that first night when you cried
to let us know the cave was cold,
I wrapped you in swaddling clothes.
Joseph and I held you,
rocked you, warmed you.

This night, this hour,
with another Joseph at my side,
I hold you,
rock you again,
swaddle you in a shroud
that is powerless to warm you.

Your crying is done.
Be with me now.
Mine has just begun.

Late in the afternoon, since it was the Day of Preparation (that is, Sabbath eve), Joseph of Arimathea, a highly respected member of the Jewish Council, came. He was one who lived expectantly, on the lookout for the kingdom of God. Working up his courage, he went to Pilate and asked for Jesus' body. Pilate questioned whether he could be dead that soon and called for the captain to verify that he was really dead. Assured by the captain, he gave Joseph the corpse.

Mark 15:42-45

JESUS IS LAID TO REST (STATION 14)

His work is done.
We still have work to do.
Lay his torn body in my tomb.

His life bought death for him.
His death bought life for us.
I gladly give him room.

Having already purchased a linen shroud, Joseph took him down, wrapped him in the shroud, placed him in a tomb that had been cut into the rock, and rolled a large stone across the opening.

Mark 15:46-47

EASTER EVENING

At any other time
Jesus would have knocked,
listened for *Come in*,
and left again
if he heard no *Welcome*.

But not tonight!
Tonight no doors or walls
were strong enough
to keep him out.
He'd earned the right
to come on over to their side
where they were locked in terror.

He stood before them now
in risen robes—
a pillar of fire leading them
across the desert of their fears,
a beacon in the stormy sea
of their floundering—
and revealed to them
the promised land: himself.

Peace, he said.
Touch my hands and feet.
Take courage. It is I!

While they were saying all this, Jesus appeared to them and said, "Peace be with you." They thought they were seeing a ghost and were scared half to death. He continued with them, "Don't be upset, and don't let all these doubting questions take over. Look at my hands; look at my feet—it's really me. Touch me. Look me over from head to toe. A ghost doesn't have muscle and bone like this." As he said this, he showed them his hands and feet.

Luke 24:36-40

FINDING MARY

Renaissance artists, knowing suffering and death
were the wages of sin, placed her in a world apart:
painted her eternally young, gave her garments
of ethereal blue, planted lilies in her ivory hands,
made her mother through a painless birth. We look
for her closer to home and find her immersed
like us in the blood and bone of humanness....

She is digging in the garden, dirt beneath her nails,
dropping trowel in fear when an angel hails her:
Mary, full of grace! She dares to ask questions—
a little nothing of a girl from a little nothing town
of which it is said that nothing good could come.
Before she assents to what God is asking,
does she imagine the neighbors hurling stones?

She and Joseph arrive in crowded Bethlehem—
House of Bread and shut doors. *Hurry, Joseph,
the baby is coming! Find something, anything!*
Inn-hospitality greets them with cold eyes, offers
a smelly cave, a borrowed manger, the steaming
breath of donkey and sheep. No midwife is there
to help young Mary give birth to her firstborn.

She and Joseph are fleeing with Jesus through
desert dangers. Wailing winds fill the night with
cries of mothers mourning murdered infant sons.
Arriving in Egypt, refugees in a strange land,
they bargain for bread and a place to sleep
in return for bricklaying, a new table or chair.
Provident Joseph always carries his tools.

Twelve years go by. After Passover
she and Joseph are returning home to Nazareth.
Where's Jesus? they wonder. *With the other boys?
No, not there…. Still at the inn? Not there either!*
After three worrisome days, they find him with the Elders
in the Temple, asking questions, giving answers.
How could you do this! she cries. *Your father and I….*

Years later, Nazareth whispers and stares at the widow
whose son has gone out of his mind. When she goes
to him in Capernaum, he lets her stand there, outside,
as he reaches out toward a ragged crowd: *You who do
my Father's will are my brothers and sisters and mother.*
She ponders the meaning of this new kind of family,
related not by blood but by obedience to the Father.

In the end, Mary stands with that other beloved disciple,
her garments soaked with Jesus' blood as he delivers
his family, born of Spirit, into her care. Mother and sister,
she midwifes us now through our births and deaths,
offering her Son on the altar of her knees.

*A good woman is hard to find,
        and worth far more than diamonds.*

*When she speaks she has something worthwhile to say,
        and she always says it kindly.
She keeps an eye on everyone in her household,
        and keeps them all busy and productive.
Her children respect and bless her;
        her husband joins in with words of praise:
"Many women have done wonderful things,
        but you've outclassed them all!"*

Proverbs 31:10, 26-29

GOD'S WORLD

Help us hear You pass
in the footfalls of a robin on the grass.
—from "Learning to Listen with Elijah"

Everything around us whispers shhhh.
We listen to the breath of God
bringing forth the world.
—from "Autumn Afternoon at Rosie's Corner"

You are at home with us here,
You whose holy presence the world cannot contain.
—from "This Holy Place"

CREATION

We listen to Your breathing
throughout the universe
and celebrate Your breath
in all these Bethlehems.

*What a wildly wonderful world, G*OD*!*
  You made it all, with Wisdom at your side,
  made earth overflow with your wonderful creations.

Psalm 104:24

"But ask the animals what they think—let them teach you;
  let the birds tell you what's going on.
Put your ear to the earth—learn the basics.
  Listen—the fish in the ocean will tell you their stories.
Isn't it clear they all know and agree
  *that G*OD *is sovereign, that he holds all things in his hand—*
Every living soul, yes, every breathing creature?

Job 12:7-10

IN GOD'S GALLERY

Some come as tourists, snapping photos
of each masterpiece. Some come to buy,
but learn the prices are sky-high.

Still others come to study, seriously,
the marks distinguishing the Master's artistry
in microbe, mountain, moon, and galaxy.

These soon have no need to look beneath
a leaf or star to read the signature there.
They recognize God's style everywhere.

All together now—applause for God!
Sing songs to the tune of his glory,
set glory to the rhythms of his praise.
Say of God, "We've never seen anything like him!"
When your enemies see you in action,
they slink off like scolded dogs.
The whole earth falls to its knees—
it worships you, sings to you,
can't stop enjoying your name and fame.

Take a good look at God's wonders—
they'll take your breath away.

Psalm 66:1-5

There's no one quite like you among the gods, O Lord,
and nothing to compare with your works.

Psalm 86:8

SONG OF PRAISE FOR MOON AND STARS

Praise to You, luminous God,
for Sister Moon who bathes the earth
in quiet light; for the motherly moon
who makes her nightly round to wish us all
a blessed sleep; for the no longer distant moon,
now marked by giant steps for humankind;
for the moon that tugs our oceans toward her,
hugs our earth with fierce or quiet tenderness.

Praise to You, luminous God,
for fields of stars that lured our ancestors
to wander through creation myths;
for stars that twinkle and tease our children
to wonder who and where *You* are;
for stars that tell us we are not the center
of the universe, that call us to contemplate
worlds beyond…and beyond…and beyond.

Praise to You, Creator of moon and stars
that light the way for all Earth-people—
all of us kinfolk, all brothers and sisters—
to trek through oceans of time and space
into Your embrace, luminous God.

Hallelujah!
Praise GOD from heaven,
     praise him from the mountaintops;
Praise him, all you his angels,
     praise him, all you his warriors,
Praise him, sun and moon,
     praise him, you morning stars;
Praise him, high heaven,
     praise him, heavenly rain clouds;
Praise, oh let them praise the name of GOD—
     he spoke the word, and there they were!
He set them in place
     from all time to eternity;
He gave his orders,
     and that's it!

Psalm 148:1-6

CREATION OF THE CROCODILE

To give her rivers company
God took a shapeless entity,
squished and squeezed repeatedly,
then opened up her hand to see
her clayful creativity.

You and I, undoubtedly,
with limited ability
to appreciate aesthetically
a crocodile's long-gevity,
would have preferred more brevity

and snipped off tail or head. Instead,
the Creator said, delightedly,
How like a log I made you be.
You fit my rivers perfectly!
and laughed and laughed infectiously.

As the crocodile adoringly
joined in God's hilarity,
its soft clay mouth grew lengthily.
With infinite sensitivity
God stopped laughing immediately.

But when you are in the vicinity
of a crocodile, watch for awhile
and you'll see God smile.

God spoke: "Swarm, Ocean, with fish and all sea life!
 Birds, fly through the sky over Earth!"
God created the huge whales,
 all the swarm of life in the waters,
And every kind and species of flying birds.
 God saw that it was good.

Genesis 1:20-22

You started the springs and rivers,
 sent them flowing among the hills.

The glory of GOD, let it last forever.
 Let GOD enjoy his creation.

Psalm 104:10-12, 31

LEARNING TO LISTEN WITH ELIJAH

Help us hear You, God,
in every tiny thing,
every whispering:

the chirp of baby birds at dawn
squirrels racing on the lawn

the crackle of thin ice
squeaking mice

maple sap dripping in spring
the whir of a hummingbird's wing

a chick pecking out of its egg
a leaf breaking off its twig

the unfolding petals of a rose
my heart beating in repose

O God, help us hear You pass
in the footfalls of a robin on the grass.

Then Elijah was told, "Go, stand on the mountain at attention before GOD. GOD will pass by."

A hurricane wind ripped through the mountains and shattered the rocks before GOD, but GOD wasn't to be found in the wind; after the wind an earthquake, but GOD wasn't in the earthquake; and after the earthquake fire, but GOD wasn't in the fire; and after the fire a gentle and quiet whisper.

When Elijah heard the quiet voice, he muffled his face with his great cloak, went to the mouth of the cave, and stood there. A quiet voice asked, "So Elijah, now tell me, what are you doing here?"

1 Kings 19:11-13

WITNESSES

Last week a flock of sparrows
congregating on a barren tree
sang spiritedly of spring's approach,
but I passed by, unbelieving.

Today I stand in awe
as a miracle of leaves unfolds
and white cherry blossoms
baptize me.

Lilacs are exuberantly purple and perfumed,
    and cherry trees fragrant with blossoms.
Oh, get up, dear friend,
    my fair and beautiful lover—come to me!

Song of Songs 2:13

Send out your Spirit and they spring to life—
    the whole countryside in bloom and blossom.

Psalm 104:30

AS A HEN GATHERS HER BROOD

Hatched only yesterday,
the chicks flit fast as Olympic
runners, radiating out
from the hen's safe circle.

"Keep close," she clucks
to her skittish brood as she scratches
with triple-clawed feet,
sending straw and grain flying.

The tiny yellow peepers dart out
and back under her, out and under.
On a nearby tree a hawk watches,
cold and calculating, biding its time.

"Jerusalem, Jerusalem, killer of prophets,
    abuser of the messengers of God!
How often I've longed to gather your children,
    gather your children like a hen,
Her brood safe under her wings—
    but you refused and turned away!
And now it's too late: You won't see me again
    until the day you say,
        'Blessed is he who comes
        in the name of God.'"

Luke 13:34-35

SUMMER RETREAT

Daybreak

The dog barks
to wake the rooster
that wakes the dawn.

The cat pads
to the woods.
I take the lake road.

At the water's edge
a fish half eaten—
an empty eye socket.

No sunrise
this morning—
that eye too is eaten.

A gull plummets,
comes up empty.
The fish was swifter.

Fossils in the rocks—
ancient fish
caught.

Silence
is a white
seashell.

Day

A tree frog croaks
in the screened-in porch,
sends me off the rocker.

A spider swings
in mid-air
far from its tree.

A wounded butterfly
lies on the road
wings tuckered out.

Darkness

Maple leaves
whisper night prayers
under a crescent moon.

In the chapel,
silent worshippers
and one loud cricket.

What a beautiful home, GOD-of-the-Angel-Armies!
    I've always longed to live in a place like this,
Always dreamed of a room in your house,
    where I could sing for joy to God-alive!

Psalm 84:1-2

All the creatures look expectantly to you
    to give them their meals on time.
You come, and they gather around;
    you open your hand and they eat from it.

Psalm 104:27-28

FOWL FIDELITY AT 5:00 A.M.

I woke to the rooster's crow—
a task given long ago
to his ancestral clay—
and wondered: though
he'll never renege on his faithful din
(being untouched by original sin)
does he ever, in some rooster way,
long for a rainy day
so he can sleep in?

Get out of bed, Jerusalem!
> *Wake up. Put your face in the sunlight.*
> *GOD's bright glory has risen for you.*
The whole earth is wrapped in darkness,
> *all people sunk in deep darkness,*
But GOD rises on you,
> *his sunrise glory breaks over you.*

Isaiah 60:1-3

Bless GOD, all creatures, wherever you are—
> *everything and everyone made by God.*

And you, O my soul, bless GOD!

Psalm 103:22

A SQUIRREL AND I AT MORNING PRAYER

The squirrel arrives at the same time as I.
It sits on the sunny side of a tree branch.
I sit watching it from my room.

It begins with a vigorous, total scratch
from head to tail, section by section.
All ye creatures, bless the Lord.

Next, the left front leg, then the right
whirs against ribs, nose, cheeks, ears.
Praise and exalt God forever.

Now the tail curves upward, rests along its back,
lifts, falls, dangles over the branch.
All ye creatures, bless the Lord.

The squirrel rests on its branch, I sit inside,
each of us praying in our own fashion.
Praise and exalt God above all forever.

Creation and creatures applaud you, GOD;
your holy people bless you.

They talk about the glories of your rule,
they exclaim over your splendor.

All eyes are on you, expectant;
you give them their meals on time.

Generous to a fault,
you lavish your favor on all creatures.

Everything GOD does is right—
the trademark on all his works is love.

GOD's there, listening for all who pray,
for all who pray and mean it.

He does what's best for those who fear him—
hears them call out, and saves them.

GOD sticks by all who love him,
but it's all over for those who don't.

My mouth is filled with GOD's praise.
Let everything living bless him,
bless his holy name from now to eternity!

Psalm 145:10-12, 15-21

PSALM RESPONSE

"Your words are sweet as honey
to my mouth," I prayed.

Instantly, a memory of chipmunk
darted in and sat behind
a broken branch beyond my prayer,
pulverizing seed with dizzying
speed and concentration.

I watched it nibbling behind the psalm,
words dribbling from my mouth.

These are the words in my mouth;
    these are what I chew on and pray.
Accept them when I place them
    on the morning altar,
O God, my Altar-Rock,
    God, Priest-of-My-Altar.

Psalm 19:14

SOLAR GRAFFITI

The morning sun, peering through
my window, saw my peace lily,
drew its leaves across the wall
and moved on.

An amateur with pen and ink,
I fumbled, trying to recall
those perfect lines so quickly drawn,
so quickly gone.

If I could learn to see like sun
I too would move around the world,
drawing peace on every wall
till earth was one.

They know nothing about peace
  and less than nothing about justice.
They make tortuously twisted roads.
  No peace for the wretch who walks down those roads!

Which means that we're a far cry from fair dealing,
  and we're not even close to right living.
We long for light but sink into darkness,
  long for brightness but stumble through the night.

Isaiah 59:8-9

GARDENS, GARDENS

When Florence, sacred city of art,
was plagued with famine,
the holy bishop filled his floral gardens
with peas and beans to feed his people.
Who would not applaud his charity!

And yet, I think he could have saved
a bit of garden-room
for a flower.
For staving off starvation,
beauty too has power.

*Was I ever so awed by the sun's brilliance
      and moved by the moon's beauty?*

Job 31:26

*Your vibrant beauty has gotten inside us—
      you've been so good to us! We're walking on air!*

Psalm 89:17

DAWN IN YOSEMITE VALLEY

A doe and fawn
acknowledge me
with a flick of their tails
and continue to feed
on winter berries
as I pass by
and move up the nave
of this vast cathedral.

They have no fear.
Like me, they've come
to worship where
Yosemite Falls
baptizes granite
with prisms of light
and the sun presides
at the altar of Half Dome.

A white-tailed deer drinks
    from the creek;
I want to drink God,
    deep draughts of God.
I'm thirsty for God-alive.
I wonder, "Will I ever make it—
    arrive and drink in God's presence?"

Psalm 42:1-2

I'm singing joyful praise to GOD.
    I'm turning cartwheels of joy to my Savior God.
Counting on GOD's *Rule to prevail,*
    I take heart and gain strength.
I run like a deer.
    I feel like I'm king of the mountain!

Habakkuk 3:18-19

FALLOWING

Today I freed the white-winged seed
tightly packed in milkweed pod
and watched them fly
to fallowing sod.

Next fall these may be seen or heard
in pod or poem, seed or word—
compressed munificence
of God.

God spoke: "Earth, green up! Grow all varieties
of seed-bearing plants,
Every sort of fruit-bearing tree."
And there it was.
Earth produced green seed-bearing plants,
all varieties,
And fruit-bearing trees of all sorts.
God saw that it was good.
It was evening, it was morning—
Day Three.

Genesis 1:11-13

TESTIMONY

The rainbow blossomed
without a sound—
no roll of thunder,
no wild exploding.

Then in an instant
the splendor was gone.
It left me there.
Bereft. Alone.

I alone was left
to witness the glory.
It is given to me
to tell the story.

Then God spoke to Noah and his sons: "I'm setting up my covenant with you that never again will everything living be destroyed by floodwaters; no, never again will a flood destroy the Earth."

God continued, "This is the sign of the covenant I am making between me and you and everything living around you and everyone living after you. I'm putting my rainbow in the clouds, a sign of the covenant between me and the Earth. From now on, when I form a cloud over the Earth and the rainbow appears in the cloud, I'll remember my covenant between me and you and everything living, that never again will floodwaters destroy all life. When the rainbow appears in the cloud, I'll see it and remember the eternal covenant between God and everything living, every last living creature on Earth."

And God said, "This is the sign of the covenant that I've set up between me and everything living on the Earth."

Genesis 9:11-17

AUTUMN AFTERNOON AT ROSIE'S CORNER

The long valley yawns before us,
spreading wide its quilted yellow,
green, gold, and ochre fields
of hay, beans, and corn.

We sit in stillness listening to
our squeaking swing,
the rustle of drying corn nearby,
the cry of a hawk riding a thermal.

Everything around us whispers *shhhhh*.
We listen to the breath of God
bringing forth the world.

Then God said, "I've given you
  every sort of seed-bearing plant on Earth
And every kind of fruit-bearing tree,
  given them to you for food.
To all animals and all birds,
  everything that moves and breathes,
I give whatever grows out of the ground for food."
  And there it was.

God looked over everything he had made;
  it was so good, so very good!
It was evening, it was morning—
Day Six.

Genesis 1:29-31

SO LATE THE LESSON

Mornings I shared toast with a chipmunk.
Evenings on the ridge, I watched the sun
bathe the Mississippi bluffs in lavender.

All week autumn crept farther up the leaves.

Returning from the woods one afternoon,
I saw a bat-like creature clinging
to the eaves above the tiny porch.

I didn't know what it was.
I thought it might attack me.
I thought I had to kill it.

Its compact body jerked as I pounded.

Its eyes stared in startled agony;
its mute mouth opened, closed,
opened, closed.

But once I had begun, I had to finish.
I tried not to think
of what it was trying to tell me.

Years later, when visiting an exhibit
of nocturnal creatures, I saw and read
about the flying squirrel.

What I killed would not have hurt me.

God spoke: "Earth, generate life! Every sort and kind:
    cattle and reptiles and wild animals—all kinds."
And there it was:
    wild animals of every kind,
Cattle of all kinds, every sort of reptile and bug.
    God saw that it was good.

God spoke: "Let us make human beings in our image, make them
    reflecting our nature
So they can be responsible for the fish in the sea,
    the birds in the air, the cattle,
And, yes, Earth itself,
    and every animal that moves on the face of Earth."

Genesis 1:24-26

DOVE

After two weeks of below-zero days,
a dove coos on the tree outside my window,
its claws securely curled around a branch.
Is it waiting for a mate? Waiting for spring?

Perhaps it's not waiting at all, content
to sit and coo in the warmth it has found,
content not to flit from branch to branch,
from tree to tree to seek more sun.

The psalms rest on my lap, unread.
Look at the birds of the air, Jesus said.

Birds find nooks and crannies in your house,
   sparrows and swallows make nests there.
They lay their eggs and raise their young,
   singing their songs in the place where we worship.
GOD-of-the-Angel-Armies! King! God!
   How blessed they are to live and sing there!

Psalm 84:3-4

"Look at the birds, free and unfettered, not tied down to a job
description, careless in the care of God. And you count far
more to him than birds."

Matthew 6:26

WINDOWS

O Holy One,
shining through
the stained glass windows
of Your world,
help us see You
in the prismed radiance
coloring the stone tiles
of our lives.

God created human beings;
*   he created them godlike,*
Reflecting God's nature.
*   He created them male and female.*
God blessed them: "Prosper! Reproduce! Fill Earth!"

Genesis 1:27

IMMORTAL, INVISIBLE

St. Francis died
almost eight hundred
years ago,
the homilist said.
St. Francis dead? No!

He lives
in caring hands
and quieting eye,
in singing stream,
flaming leaf,
and flowering sky.

The death that separates
him from us
is so thin!
He moves among us
freely here,
unlimited by skin.

Eight days later, his disciples were again in the room. This time Thomas was with them. Jesus came through the locked doors, stood among them, and said, "Peace to you."

Then he focused his attention on Thomas. "Take your finger and examine my hands. Take your hand and stick it in my side. Don't be unbelieving. Believe."

Thomas said, "My Master! My God!"

John 20:26-28

ANTHONY DE MELLO'S WORKSHOP ON PRAYER

Sculptor of words, he hammered
and chiseled a solid block of content,
quickly, deftly, precisely disclosing
the shape of his teaching.

We hearers, awed by its power and beauty
even as it stood in the rough,
thought we understood, more or less,
and waited for further embellishments—
the decorative figures, twists, curves
we'd come to expect of an artist.

But he, having seen perfection as God's
apprentice, knew it lay not in more, but in less.
So he hammered and chiseled, with humor
and conviction, lightly, relentlessly,
till the marble heart of the message appeared—
smooth, solid, one-worded: Awareness.

It was too simple for us to comprehend.
We asked for further explanation.
Obligingly, he smiled, repeated:
Awareness. Awareness. Awareness.

From the time I was young, before I sinned for the first time, I sought wisdom openly in my prayer. I demanded it right in front of the Temple. Right down to the present day I inquired after it; eventually it opened like a flower, like a grape before its time....

Come to me, those who don't know; gather round, those who want to know. Why have you been so slow to apply to the School of Wisdom when your minds thirst for knowledge? Here are a few tips. Put yourself on an extreme budget. Commit yourself to the program. Don't let your mind wander. Next thing you know, you'll have found wisdom. You can see, I've worked at it for a while and found time to reflect. Higher education costs a lot of money, but you'll find much gold in your studies. Relax your mind in the Lord; keep your prayers simple. Work yourself silly in your own good time. The Lord will reward you nicely in his own good time.

Sirach 51:18,31-38

MISSIONARY MOTHER

Her missionary Sister-daughter
has been riding burros to mountain villages
in Peru for thirty years.

The old mother is getting closer
to the day she'll become the oldest
she will ever be.

The son drops by to visit. *Mom, we're making*
a CD for Sister. We need you on it.
Give her a little message.

A message? What can I say?
She looks nervously at the unfamiliar machine.
You tell her something for me.

The recorder begins to listen.
What do you want me to tell her? the son asks.
She wipes her hands on her apron.

Tell her I pray for her.
She gets a cup from the cupboard.
The recorder listens.

Tell her I pray for her in the morning.
She fills the cup with coffee.
And again at noon.

She sets the cup in front of her son.
Tell her I pray for her every night....
Just tell her I pray for her all the time.

Later, when Sister-daughter's burro
slips on the steep, rocky trail
and goes down on its knees,

she sees the naked sky surrounding her,
the tree tops far below,
and hangs on tight to her mother's prayers.

"Can a mother forget the infant at her breast,
walk away from the baby she bore?
But even if mothers forget,
I'd never forget you—never."

Isaiah 49:15

"I made all this! I own all this!"
GOD's Decree.
"But there is something I'm looking for:
a person simple and plain,
reverently responsive to what I say."

Isaiah 66:2

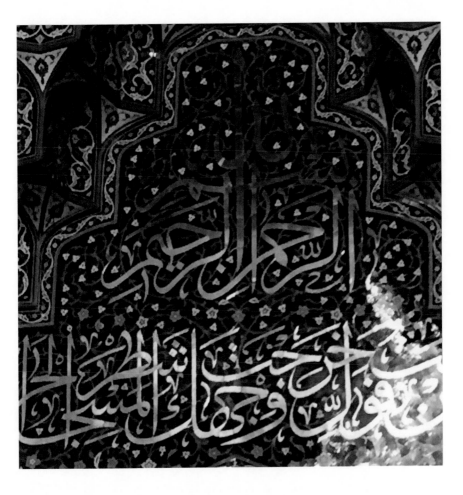

WHAT GOD LOOKS LIKE

(an incident told by Sister of Charity Peggy O'Neill and reported by Jacob Scobey-Polacheck in The Catholic Herald, *Milwaukee, Wisconsin, May 21, 2015)*

The Salvadoran boy was no older
than nine or ten. He picked up a banana
that had fallen off a bus, peeled it,
raised it to his lips, stopped.

An old man stood nearby. The boy
walked over and gave him the fruit.
Sister pushed her way to the boy
and asked, "Is he your father?"

"No," he replied as he began
to chew on the peel.

"Your grandfather, then?" she pursued.

"No," he answered again, still chewing.

"Then why?" she asked, almost fiercely,
unable to believe such virtue in one
so young. (How many years
had it taken her to bear such fruit?)

"He looked hungrier than I," the boy
said simply, smiling. He had attended
the school of hunger and learned
to distinguish between its varying degrees.

"I looked at him, chewing the banana peel,"
Sister concluded, "and saw the face of God."

"Then the King will say to those on his right, 'Enter, you who are blessed by my Father! Take what's coming to you in this kingdom. It's been ready for you since the world's foundation. And here's why:

> I was hungry and you fed me,
> I was thirsty and you gave me a drink,
> I was homeless and you gave me a room,
> I was shivering and you gave me clothes,
> I was sick and you stopped to visit,
> I was in prison and you came to me.'

"Then those 'sheep' are going to say, 'Master, what are you talking about? When did we ever see you hungry and feed you, thirsty and give you a drink? And when did we ever see you sick or in prison and come to you?' Then the King will say, 'I'm telling the solemn truth: Whenever you did one of these things to someone overlooked or ignored, that was me—you did it to me.'"

Matthew 25:34-40

A PILGRIM'S PROGRESS

That precarious April day when I
began to be, I was as yet all promise,
one-celled only, the nearest I could get
to being nothing. I had no ears to hear
the mother-drum above me send a rush
of blood down a nearby artery,

nor eyes to see the outside world awaking—
newborn calves tottering toward their mother's
milk, robins snatching rain-washed worms,
chicks in corrugated cardboard boxes
peeping all the way from hatchery
to post office to backyard brooder house.

By mid-October I'd grown ears. Perhaps
human voices, laughter, singing found
their way inside the warm, protective walls
surrounding me. But I as yet possessed
no consciousness, no power to wonder if
there was a world outside awaiting me.

Now in this middle life, when Mozart music
lifts me into space, or snow festoons
the cedars, or a child tugs me out
to see the salamanders she discovered
in a window well, I wonder if
my sudden joy can be an intimation
of a life beyond this dazzling one.

Oh yes, you shaped me first inside, then out;
  you formed me in my mother's womb.
I thank you, High God—you're breathtaking!
    Body and soul, I am marvelously made!
    I worship in adoration—what a creation!
You know me inside and out,
    you know every bone in my body;
You know exactly how I was made, bit by bit,
    how I was sculpted from nothing into something.
Like an open book, you watched me grow from conception to birth;
    all the stages of my life were spread out before you,
The days of my life all prepared
    before I'd even lived one day.

Psalm 139:13-16

AWAKENING

Annie has started school and I, at four,
am free to explore the farmyard, barn,
and sheds alone. A skinny cat pads intently
toward the old tool shed. I follow her inside.

She climbs a rusty plow and jumps down
onto a broken car seat where high-pitched
mewing greets her. Squirming kittens tumble
over and under one another, stepping

heedlessly on ears and still unopened eyes.
The mewing stops as tiny paws begin to knead
and mouths to drink in sync. The mother cat
purrs contentedly in rhythm to my petting.

Above me, in the semi-darkness, pigeons
quietly coo and flutter their wings.
Light filters through a dusty window.
My young soul milks the cool serenity.

I'm ready, God, so ready,
        ready from head to toe,
Ready to sing, ready to raise a tune:
        "Wake up, soul!
Wake up, harp! wake up, lute!
        Wake up, you sleepyhead sun!"

Psalm 57:7-8

ONE SUMMER NIGHT

Till rising and gliding out, I wander'd off by myself
In the mystical moist night-air, and from time to time,
Look'd up in perfect silence at the stars.—Walt Whitman

One summer night, this child of the universe
carried flashlight, alarm clock, star maps,
and blanket out beyond yard-light and trees
to a field fertile with darkness, there to watch
the majestic march of stars throughout the night.

The Milky Way was a dim trail that stretched
across the sky. The summer constellations—
Cassiopeia, Lyra the Harp, the Southern Cross,
the Pleiades—shone in the panoply of stars.
An occasional meteor streaked across the heavens.
She consulted her star maps, set the alarm, turned off
the flashlight, and lay awake drinking in the glory.

When the alarm woke her at 2:00 a.m., the starry sky
had revolved to winter, as the star map had promised.
Orion the Hunter and Leo the Lion blazed above her
as they had shone above this Iowa field a century ago,
perhaps comforting a lonely young man when he saw
the familiar stars he had known across the ocean,
back home where his parents still lived.

She thought of that man who became her grandfather
and of the unknown ancestors before him—people
who had lived in lands that became Germany, Austria,
Bohemia, Hungary; people who at night had sat beneath
these stars, singing songs and telling stories in languages
she would not have understood. She thought of the whole
human family who had gazed and would gaze at the splendor
above her, and quietly adored the infinite God who created
these stars, who created her ancestors, who created her.

I look up at your macro-skies, dark and enormous,
     your handmade sky-jewelry,
Moon and stars mounted in their settings.
     Then I look at my micro-self and wonder,
Why do you bother with us?
     Why take a second look our way?

Yet we've so narrowly missed being gods,
     bright with Eden's dawn light.

Psalm 8:3-5

MINISTRY

Take care of yourselves, they warned us.
If you burn out, you're no good to anyone.
But I think of you at home in Capernaum.

No one stood at your door to admit only those
who had made advanced reservations.
You welcomed everyone: *Come in,* you said,
all you who labor and are heavily burdened.

They took you at your word—trampled
your yard, crowded your house.
One day even your roof had to go.
How are we to learn from you to say no?

Jesus dismissed him with strict orders: "Say nothing to anyone. Take the offering for cleansing that Moses prescribed and present yourself to the priest. This will validate your healing to the people." But as soon as the man was out of earshot, he told everyone he met what had happened, spreading the news all over town. So Jesus kept to out-of-the-way places, no longer able to move freely in and out of the city. But people found him, and came from all over.

Mark 1:43-45

After a few days, Jesus returned to Capernaum, and word got around that he was back home. A crowd gathered, jamming the entrance so no one could get in or out. He was teaching the Word. They brought a paraplegic to him, carried by four men. When they weren't able to get in because of the crowd, they removed part of the roof and lowered the paraplegic on his stretcher.... Then Jesus went again to walk alongside the lake. Again a crowd came to him, and he taught them.

Mark 2:1-4, 13

JACOB AT PENIEL

I have seen God face to face,
yet my life has been spared.—Genesis 32:31

I keep this story of struggle on file
for times when I want to resort to denial
or am otherwise tempted to give up the trial.

But Jacob stayed behind by himself, and a man wrestled with him until daybreak. When the man saw that he couldn't get the best of Jacob as they wrestled, he deliberately threw Jacob's hip out of joint.

The man said, "Let me go; it's daybreak."

Jacob said, "I'm not letting you go 'til you bless me."

The man said, "What's your name?"

He answered, "Jacob."

The man said, "But no longer. Your name is no longer Jacob. From now on it's Israel (God-Wrestler); you've wrestled with God and you've come through."

Jacob asked, "And what's your name?"

The man said, "Why do you want to know my name?" And then, right then and there, he blessed him.

Jacob named the place Peniel (God's Face) because, he said, "I saw God face-to-face and lived to tell the story!"

Genesis 32:24-30

ON A DARK NIGHT

"How does one hush one's house…?"
—Jessica Powers, in response to the poem
by St. John of the Cross: "En una noche oscura"

How does one hush one's house? the poet asks.
How does one shush the loud, incessant tasks
that flood across the threshold of the mind
and drown the stillness one had hoped to find
inside the sanctuary of one's inner room?
How does one shut windows when the boom
and clatter of mental talk intrude
to rob the place of peaceful solitude?

How does one resolutely show the door
to guests who've taken over every floor
and filled the house with anger, jealousy?
How does one restore tranquility?
How does one hush the din?
How does one hear the quiet within?

*"Blessed be God, who has given peace to his people Israel just
as he said he'd do. Not one of all those good and wonderful
words that he spoke through Moses has misfired."*

1 Kings 8:56

*He rescued me from enemy anger,
    he pulled me from the grip of upstarts,
He saved me from the bullies.*

Psalm 18:48

*Don't be quick to fly off the handle.
Anger boomerangs. You can spot a fool by the lumps on his head.*

Ecclesiastes 7:9

FARMER GOD

I am a field
on which You scatter seed.
If some hungry sparrows
come to feed
upon some grains before
they germinate, let it be—
sparrows, too, depend upon
Your prodigality.

But, O my God, allow
enough of me to grow
and ripen in Your summer love.
Before the harvest mow,
let warm winds blow
across this field of wheat
that I may show Your beauty
at Your feet.

As they went from town to town, a lot of people joined in and traveled along. He addressed them, using this story: "A farmer went out to sow his seed. Some of it fell on the road; it was tramped down and the birds ate it. Other seed fell in the gravel; it sprouted, but withered because it didn't have good roots. Other seed fell in the weeds; the weeds grew with it and strangled it. Other seed fell in rich earth and produced a bumper crop.

"Are you listening to this? Really listening?"

Luke 8:4-8

LIKE A MOTHER HEN

There was a day
you cried over Jerusalem
and yearned like a mother hen
to gather the chicks
under your wing.

Mothering Jesus,
brood over me now,
that when I arrive
at the dark wall of death,
I'll see it to be
the mere outer shell of me,
meant to be pecked open.

Help me then to thrust
again and again in trust,
until the shell is broken.

Keep me safe, O God,
I've run for dear life to you.
I say to GOD, "Be my Lord!"
Without you, nothing makes sense.

Psalm 16:1-2

When I get really afraid
I come to you in trust.

Psalm 56:3

AGING

I'm still running in time,
more on the mark,
more sure, more set,
though not yet ready to go.

I'm running that race
in place, attentive
to breathing—
the yin and yang of it,

becoming aware
that yesterday's exhalations
have been purified
by green trees;

becoming aware
that the rot of dead flowers
has been transformed
into peas, carrots, roses;

becoming aware
of the garbage I give You,
greening God,
and what You make of it;

becoming aware
of what You make of death—
how You transform
the necessary rot of it;

becoming aware
of Your purifying
breath in me.
Of immortality.

I run for dear life to G<small>OD</small>,
    I'll never live to regret it.

You keep me going when times are tough—
    my bedrock, G<small>OD</small>, since my childhood.
I've hung on you from the day of my birth,
    the day you took me from the cradle;
        I'll never run out of praise.
Many gasp in alarm when they see me,
    but you take me in stride.

Just as each day brims with your beauty,
    my mouth brims with praise.
But don't turn me out to pasture when I'm old
    or put me on the shelf when I can't pull my weight.

I'll write the book on your righteousness,
    talk up your salvation the livelong day,
        never run out of good things to write or say.

Now I'm telling the world your wonders
I'll keep at it until I'm old and gray.
God, don't walk off and leave me
until I get out the news
Of your strong right arm to this world,
news of your power to the world yet to come,
Your famous and righteous
ways, O God.
God, you've done it all!
Who is quite like you?
You, who made me stare trouble in the face,
Turn me around;
Now let me look life in the face.

Psalm 71:1, 5-9, 15, 18-20

EASTER CREDO

I believe that during a storm at sea,
when everything is roaring out of tune
and giant fists of waves loom above me,
I'll hear you call: *Take courage. It is I.*

I believe that when I run to look for you
among the tombs, I'll hear a voice—
strange and yet familiar—call my name,
and turn to find you smiling.

I believe that if I try to hide
behind my fearful, childish walls,
you'll scarcely notice, easily pass through.
I believe in Easter!

God holds me head and shoulders
　　above all who try to pull me down.
I'm headed for his place to offer anthems
　　that will raise the roof!
Already I'm singing God-songs;
　　I'm making music to God.

Psalm 27:6

Meanwhile, the boat was far out to sea when the wind came up against them and they were battered by the waves. At about four o'clock in the morning, Jesus came toward them walking on the water. They were scared out of their wits. "A ghost!" they said, crying out in terror.

But Jesus was quick to comfort them. "Courage, it's me. Don't be afraid."

Matthew 14:24-27

After she said this, she turned away and saw Jesus standing there. But she didn't recognize him.

Jesus spoke to her, "Woman, why do you weep? Who are you looking for?"

She, thinking that he was the gardener, said, "Mister, if you took him, tell me where you put him so I can care for him."

Jesus said, "Mary."

Turning to face him, she said in Hebrew, "Rabboni!" meaning "Teacher!"

Later on that day, the disciples had gathered together, but, fearful of the Jews, had locked all the doors in the house. Jesus entered, stood among them, and said, "Peace to you." Then he showed them his hands and side.

The disciples, seeing the Master with their own eyes, were exuberant. Jesus repeated his greeting: "Peace to you. Just as the Father sent me, I send you."

John 20:14-16, 19-21

I AM YOUR GOD

I AM Light,
Creator of fire,
exploding into more than
a hundred billion galaxies,
each with billions
of spinning stars,
in one of them
your sun spinning,
your earth spinning.

I AM Breath
breathing forth creatures
that swim, crawl, walk,
fly, filling the seas,
land, and sky of Earth.

I AM Womb-love
birthing Earth-persons
made in my image,
each uniquely gifted
to show who I AM.

I AM Heart
loving you, dear child.
When your Earth-end nears,
do not be afraid!
I will guide you
through the abyss.

I AM your Bliss.

High heavens, sing!
    G OD *has done it.*
Deep earth, shout!
        And you mountains, sing!
        A forest choir of oaks and pines and cedars!
G OD *has redeemed Jacob.*
G OD*'s glory is on display in Israel.*

G OD, *your Redeemer,*
        who shaped your life in your mother's womb, says:
"I am G OD. *I made all that is.*
        With no help from you I spread out the skies
        and laid out the earth."

Isaiah 44:23-24

As parents feel for their children,
    GOD feels for those who fear him
He knows us inside and out,
    keeps in mind that we're made of mud.
Men and women don't live very long;
    like wildflowers they spring up and blossom,
But a storm snuffs them out just as quickly,
    leaving nothing to show they were here.
GOD's love, though, is ever and always,
    eternally present to all who fear him,
Making everything right for them and their children
    as they follow his Covenant ways
    and remember to do whatever he said.

Psalm 103:15-18

EUCHARISTIC CHAPEL

St. Joseph Retreat, Baileys Harbor, Wisconsin

In this
circled chapel
everything converges
toward the tabernacle resting
on its granite stand, rock-bottom
witness of God's constancy. We sit on
circled chairs, listening to the windowed
waves of wheat and flowing water, prisms
playing on the tiled floor, and wrought iron
gate whose rounded O of silo opens toward
the Wheat within Its golden granary. We
sit in silence, listening to the Bread,
unleavened, waiting to be eaten,
that It may rise in us.
We sit still.

During the meal, Jesus took and blessed the bread, broke it, and gave it to his disciples:

> *Take, eat.*
> *This is my body.*

Taking the cup and thanking God, he gave it to them:

> *Drink this, all of you.*
> *This is my blood,*
> *God's new covenant poured out for many people*
> *   for the forgiveness of sins.*

Matthew 26:26-28

PRESENCE

It is I who wave from fields of wheat,
I who greet you on the street,
I who come to your house to eat,
I who bathe your tired feet.

If you hide from me, I will find you.
I am in front and behind you,
beneath you, around you, above you.
It is I who love you.

It is I who ripen grapes on the vine,
I who offer you bread and wine,
I who stand in the same soup line.
I am human. I am divine.

If you hide from me, I will find you.
I am in front and behind you,
beneath you, around you, above you.
It is I who love you.

It is I who made best wine from water,
I who healed a son and a daughter,
I who am with you whenever you falter,
I who share my life at the altar.

If you hide from me, I will find you.
I am in front and behind you,
beneath you, around you, above you.
It is I who love you.

You know when I leave and when I get back;
*   I'm never out of your sight.*
You know everything I'm going to say
*   before I start the first sentence.*
I look behind me and you're there,
*   then up ahead and you're there, too—*
*   your reassuring presence, coming and going.*
This is too much, too wonderful—
*   I can't take it all in!*

Is there any place I can go to avoid your Spirit?
*   to be out of your sight?*
If I climb to the sky, you're there!
*   If I go underground, you're there!*
If I flew on morning's wings
*   to the far western horizon,*
You'd find me in a minute—
*   you're already there waiting!*
Then I said to myself, "Oh, he even sees me in the dark!
*   At night I'm immersed in the light!"*
It's a fact: darkness isn't dark to you;
*   night and day, darkness and light, they're all the same to you.*

Psalm 139:4-12

THIS HOLY PLACE

Here in this holy place,
this beautiful house we built for You,
we raise our voices praising You,
God, Artist-Builder of the universe.

You are at home with us here,
You whose holy presence the world cannot contain.
We are Your people, a mosaic formed
like many colored stones into community.

You nourish us with Word and Food at this table,
as You send us forth to share the daily Bread
You offer to a world hungry for Your love.

Young and old, we sing our joyful praise to You
for centuries of days
in this holy place where You are at home.

One day spent in your house, this beautiful place of worship,
*   beats thousands spent on Greek island beaches.*
I'd rather scrub floors in the house of my God
*   than be honored as a guest in the palace of sin.*

Psalm 84:10-11

Your love, GOD, is my song, and I'll sing it!
*   I'm forever telling everyone how faithful you are.*
I'll never quit telling the story of your love—
*   how you built the cosmos*
*   and guaranteed everything in it.*
Your love has always been our lives' foundation,
*   your fidelity has been the roof over our world.*

Psalm 89:1-2

The Word became flesh and blood,
*   and moved into the neighborhood.*
We saw the glory with our own eyes,
*   the one-of-a-kind glory,*
*   like Father, like Son,*
Generous inside and out,
*   true from start to finish.*

John 1:14

SCRIPTURE INDEX

Psalm

1 Samuel

Sirach

Song of Songs

ACKNOWLEDGMENTS

My thanks to the editors of the following publications in which these poems first appeared. Occasionally, the original title has been changed.

Anglican Theological Review: "Moving On"

Christianity and Literature: "Gardens, Gardens"

Cross Currents: "Anthony de Mello's Workshop on Prayer"

Edna St. Vincent Millay; Bristol Banner Books, Bristol, IN, John H. Morgan, editor: "Solar Graffiti"

Emmanuel Magazine: "Eucharistic Chapel"

Goose River Anthology 2016, Goose River Press; Deborah J. Benner, editor: "Autumn Afternoon at Rosie's Corner"

National Catholic Reporter: "Abraham and Sarah"; "Fowl Fidelity at 5 a.m."; "Jonah Thinks Things Over"; "Windows"

Review for Religious: "Jesus Dies (Station 12)"; "A Disciple Reflects on the Tempest"; "Dove"; "Farmer God"; "Fi(ni)shing School"; "God's Gamble"; "Jesus Falls (Station 9)"

School Sisters of St. Francis: "This Holy Place." The poem is the text for a choral piece commissioned for the centennial celebration of St. Joseph Convent Chapel, Milwaukee, set to music by Edwin T. Childs. The text was published in the congregation magazine, *Alive with the Call of the Gospel,* and other places related to the centennial. The title of this collection is taken from the last line of the poem.

Sisters Today: "Psalm Response"

Song of Saint Francis: Edition du Signe, Strassbourg; Sister Janet Petersen, OSF, editor: "Immortal, Invisible"; "Song of Praise of Moon and Stars"

St. Anthony Messenger: "Creation of the Crocodile"; "On the Way"; *"Pietà"*; "Witnesses"; "Let the Children Come to Me"

Time of Singing: "Fallowing"; "How Does One Hush One's House?"; "Missionary Mother"

Wisconsin Poets' Calendar 2015, "Gardens, Gardens"

ABOUT THE AUTHOR

Sister Irene Zimmerman, OSF, grew up on a farm near Westphalia, Iowa, where she attended school taught by the School Sisters of St. Francis. After high school, she joined that international congregation, which is noted for promoting a love of the fine arts in the classroom, as well as encouraging its members to develop their own artistic talents.

She began her ministry as a high school teacher of English and French. Later, she changed careers to serve in various clerical staff positions at the congregation's international office and at Alverno College, both located in Milwaukee. She also served for three years in Germany in a school operated by sisters of the order's European province. In her final years of active ministry, Sister Irene lived and worked at a popular retreat center in Door County, Wisconsin, where her volunteer services included offering a reflective hour of reading her scriptural poetry to the retreatants, along with leading the music for the daily and Sunday liturgies.

Early during her teaching career, Sister Irene was encouraged by a sister-colleague, herself a poet, who told her she had some poetic talent and should "work at developing those God-given gifts." Now retired in Milwaukee, Sister Irene continues to write and present her poetry, sing in church choirs, and enjoy God's Word and World. *Where God Is at Home* is her fifth book of poetry.

ABOUT THE PHOTOGRAPHER

James Stephen Behrens, OCSO, served as a priest of the Archdiocese of Newark for over twenty years before becoming a Trappist monk of the Monastery of the Holy Spirit in Conyers, Georgia. Father Behrens is the author of the *Portraits of Grace: Images and Words from the Monastery of the Holy Spirit*, as well as *Grace Revisited*, a book which combines two award-winning books: *Memories of Grace* and *Grace Is Everywhere: Reflections of an Aspiring Monk*. His photographs were featured in *Planet of Grace* by Bernadette McCarver Syder and his stories have appeared in ACTA's *Hidden Presence* and *Christmas Presence*. He has also contributed to the *National Catholic Reporter* and writes a column for *The Georgia Bulletin*.

ABOUT THE PHOTOGRAPHS

POETRY & POETS
FROM ACTA PUBLICATIONS

ALSO FROM ACTA PUBLICATIONS